Point of order!

A DOCUMENTARY OF THE

Produced by

DAVID T. BAZELON, EDITORIAL CONSULTANT

Point of Order!

ARMY-McCARTHY HEARINGS

Emile de Antonio and Daniel Talbot

W · W · NORTON & COMPANY, INC. · NEW YORK

FIRST EDITION

Film material is from Columbia Broadcasting System, Inc.
television Kinescopes.

Library of Congress Catalog Card No. 64-18677

Published simultaneously in the Dominion of
Canada by George J. McLeod Limited, Toronto

PRINTED IN THE UNITED STATES OF AMERICA

Introduction

Point of Order!*—both the startling film* (taken from the files of CBS News) *and this book authentically portraying the film—is the rendering of the Army-McCarthy Hearings held in the spring of 1954. These Hearings, which consumed the attention of the nation for thirty-six days, were at once the glaring moment of truth in the career of Senator Joe McCarthy and as well perhaps the greatest political spectacle of American history. This was because they were televised—and because the television camera, for the first time, acted as an independent force in our history.*

For those who remember, the name of Joe McCarthy need only be mentioned to be appreciated. Likewise the televised Hearings in which he confronted the American people with such terrifying intimacy. But ten years have passed, and the details of the event have faded—only the great essence remains lodged in the memory of those who lived through the television experience of the Hearings. For those who did not, some background explanation of the setting and the circumstance is even more obviously called for.

Who was McCarthy and what were the Hearings?

SENATOR JOE MCCARTHY

He was at one time so important that the man himself and what he stood for constituted a phenomenon known as "McCarthyism." It grew to be the dominant political phenomenon of the day.

It all began about a month after Alger Hiss had finally been convicted of perjury in 1950. The Junior Senator from Wisconsin, who was elected in 1946 at the age of thirty-seven, had not yet distinguished himself from any other first-term senators or, indeed, from the general run of people making a career of politics. Then he delivered a speech in Wheeling, West Virginia, on February 9, 1950. He waved some papers—this was to become his trademark—and suggested that the State Department was in the hands of the Communists. Thus began the most meteoric political career in our history.

The fuel for this engine was printer's ink. McCarthy captured the headlines and held them in a vise of continuing and startling accusations for nearly five years. There was a McCarthy story almost every day, certainly several every week. Almost everything he said and did was news in every paper across the country. And mostly what he did was to accuse individuals in the federal government of being Communists, or of having been Communists, or of having associated with Communists, or of being "soft" on them or "coddling" them. For the most part, the accusation and the innuendo were never overtaken by the facts of the case, certainly not any legal evidentiary facts of the case. One can still get a good argument going today on the question of whether McCarthy ever really exposed a single real Communist.

But at the time, accusation alone was quite sufficient—and it was clearly the essence of McCarthyism. With our present hindsight, most people now believe that the most important consideration is not whether or how many of the individuals accused were actual Communists, but just why the American people credited so many of the accusations at the time and were so caught up in the on-going accusatory process. Anyway, they were. And this was McCarthy's power. It was considerable, and it is hardly an exaggeration to say that he functioned for a time as a supplemental form of government in the United States—as you will see in the course of reading this transcript of the film Point of Order!

Mostly it was the mood of the times that carried McCarthy to the pinnacle of power he had reached when the Army-McCarthy Hearings began in April 1954. The deep suspicion and readiness to believe McCarthy's accusations were sustained by the fact that there were a good number of admitted ex-Communists around who had in fact been connected with the federal government in the past. (Some of these people were in the accusing business themselves.) Also, there was a growing accumulation of facts concerning the effectiveness of Soviet espionage, and the employment of local Communists in carrying it out. All in all, enough genuine fact on which to build a mountain of uncritical accusation. And few remembered or seemed to care that it was not against the law to be a Communist, much less to have been one in the past, that it was not per se *an act of treason. In McCarthy's hands, any past act of association with Communists, or even any sympathy for them, became an act of "implied treason." He operated a star-chamber in newsprint in which he accused, judged, and convicted numerous individuals of this homemade crime. For his purposes the term "Fifth Amendment Communist" was invented, such a person being anyone who invoked his Constitutional privilege against incriminating himself under questioning by McCarthy's Permanent Investigating Subcommittee.*

The deepest level of the mood that made McCarthyism possible was that created by the emotional backwash of World War II. One should recall the great hopes involved in the grand alliance against Hitler—which were cruelly transgressed almost as the postwar world began. A deep and enduring conflict with the Soviet Union emerged; the facts of Soviet atomic espionage during the war itself; and the utterly new and absolute horror of The Bomb. All these terrible and disappointing events joined to create a pervasive mood, a postwar nightmare mood, a national spasm of dismay.

All this was McCarthyism, and no one knew where it might end. Certainly no one knew when the Army-McCarthy Hearings began in April 1954.

THE ARMY-MCCARTHY HEARINGS:

By the time of the presidential election of 1952, less than three years after the Wheeling speech, McCarthy was a major political force in the major political effort to turn the Democrats out. They had been accused of "twenty years of treason" and, in a sweeping non sequitur, *McCarthy and his doings were the proof of the proposition. But when General Eisenhower was elected, the Democratic (or, as both Eisenhower and McCarthy said, "Democrat") "traitors" were no longer in control, which posed a problem for McCarthy.*

He could have closed up shop, or gone into another line of business; but he did not. As a consequence, an eventual collision between himself and the new Republican administration became inevitable. Where the State Department had been the primary object of attack under the Democrats, it was in the Army that McCarthy finally concentrated his search for Communist infection under the Republicans. And it was the Army that finally set up the new administration's line of resistance to a rampaging McCarthyism that could not distinguish between a good Republican and a bad Democratic administration.

After a lengthy investigation of supposed espionage at a top-secret radar center at Fort Monmouth, New Jersey, McCarthy turned his attention in January 1954 to the case of Dr. Irving Peress, a dentist who had been drafted and stationed at Camp Kilmer. Dr. Peress, after his induction, had refused to answer certain items contained in an Army loyalty questionnaire. Later, being subpoenaed to appear before McCarthy's investigating subcommittee, he pleaded the Fifth Amendment. When Dr. Peress thereafter applied for and received an honorable discharge, McCarthy became "infuriated" and accused the Army of a "conspiracy" (according to a recent retelling of the story by former President Eisenhower).

And then the fatal mistake was made. Following up the Peress matter, McCarthy called in Brigadier General Ralph Zwicker, a decorated war hero. Testifying under instructions, Zwicker was not able to satisfy McCarthy—who was in fact demanding too much, including a court-martial of Peress, which was impossible in any event. Then McCarthy exploded during the hearing into a personal attack on Zwicker, roughing him up verbally and humiliating him. In this one act, whether or not he knew it at the time, McCarthy had taken on the full power of the elite officer corps of the Army. One of their own had been mortally insulted, and a generation of living West Point ideology turned against the all-powerful Communist-hunter from Wisconsin.

The Army counterattack centered, however, not on the defense of a general but on the career of a private. He was a very important private named G. David Schine, a young man whose family owned a chain of hotels. His crucial importance derived from his very close friendship with Roy M. Cohn, McCarthy's chief counsel. Cohn had brought Schine into the McCarthy investigating group as an "expert" on Communist subversion (he was in his early twenties) and the two young men had taken a whirlwind junket through Europe "exposing" subversive influence in the International Information Administration. This trip made world headlines, and is generally considered to have been the most bizarre and bitterly comic episode in the entire phenomenon of McCarthyism. It occurred, incidentally, just one year before the beginning of the Army-McCarthy Hearings.

In July 1953, Schine received a draft notice; in November he was inducted and sent to Fort Dix for basic training. Cohn bestirred himself to secure special attention for his special friend.

Under the direction of Sherman Adams (President Eisenhower's jack-of-all-trades) and prior to the Zwicker affair, the Army had been preparing a memorandum setting forth its view of Cohn's efforts on Schine's behalf. The Army counterattack began with the release of this memorandum to select individuals within the government, and then to the press. McCarthy's response was immediate and explosive. General Eisenhower has characterized it this way: "At a press conference on the 12th of March he called the report 'blackmail,' and counterattacked with an accusation that Secretary Stevens was trying to divert the investigation to the Air Force and Navy." He also claimed that Schine was being held by the Army as a "hostage." The circus-train of the Army-McCarthy Hearings was then and there on the rails and rolling.

The Hearings were unique in the conception of their formal structure—and of course beyond the unique, if that is possible, in the way they actually worked out. In a formal way, they were a special hearing before McCarthy's own Special Subcommittee on Investigations, held to hear and report on the charges and countercharges that had been exchanged between McCarthy and the Army. Senator Karl E. Mundt of South Dakota, ranking Republican member of the subcommittee, occupied the chair temporarily vacated by McCarthy. (The Democratic minority of the subcommittee, which had been boycotting it since the summer of 1953 because of the Chairman's tactics, returned for the occasion.) Since individuals were named in support of or along with the charges and countercharges, the proceedings began with half an aspect of a trial, as well as a fact-finding or peace-making enterprise. It was certainly far out of the ordinary run of Senatorial business. How far out, only the event itself was to tell.

From the legal viewpoint, taken either as legislative or judicial proceedings, the Hearings were a shambles. The lawyer from Boston who represented the Army later said, "a good many irrelevancies were enthusiastically pursued." Irrelevancies, as a lawyer would identify them, dominated the proceedings. They also determined the outcome. Their pursuit turned out to be a superb vehicle for the exposure of personality, motive, method, character—which were indeed the "real" issues of the case and the stuff of a new form of political drama.

In the end, everyone played to the camera. There was very likely little chance under any circumstances that the collision between Senator Joe McCarthy and the United States Army could have been choreographed with optimum decorum. But the television camera—backed up by twenty million voters—made of the encounter something absolutely unique in American law and politics (and entertainment as well). There were two million words of testimony in the Hearings, delivered over thirty-six days from April 22 through June 16, 1954; but more important by far were the 188 hours of visual exposure which accompanied this verbal flow. There is no question but that it changed the history of this country.

It would be anticipating too much of the book that follows to attempt further to background or characterize the course of the inimitable Army-McCarthy Hearings. They were, in a fabulously exact sense, the greatest political show on earth. The passage of time has altered this fact not at all.

Joe McCarthy often began his vote-gathering speeches around the country by saying, "It's good to get out of Washington and back to the United States." Point Of Order! *is the brilliantly assembled story of what happened when the United States came to Washington—by means of television—for a visit with Joe McCarthy.*

David T. Bazelon

Washington, D.C., February 1964.

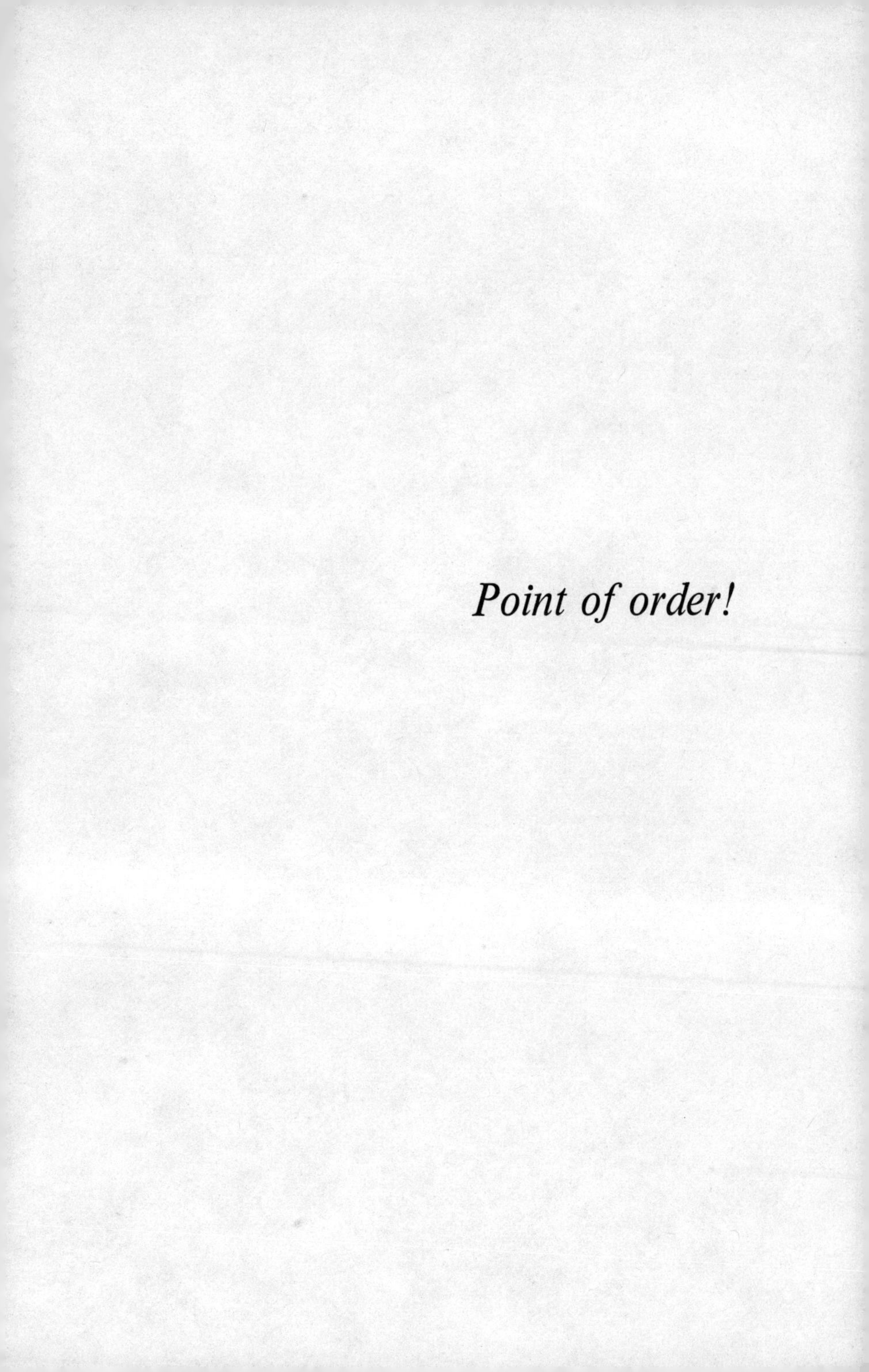

Point of order!

Cast of Characters

One of the best things that had ever happened to me in my life was my opportunity for service in the United States Army in two World Wars.

I've never filed a brief. I've never drawn a complaint. I'm strictly a Washington-type lawyer.

I came down from Boston in the guise of a simple trial lawyer. I supposed I'd try to think up some questions to ask witnesses and then, if I didn't like the answer, ask another one.

Presiding over these hearings is a responsibility which I do not welcome.

To the best of my ability I am pursuing this investigation in order to develop the facts.

We are performing a public duty, a public trust, one of the most disagreeable ones I've ever had to perform in the course of my public service.

I have no interest in life that surpasses my great concern for the vitality of our armed forces.

I am a Private in the United States Army. I have received many orders that are quite unusual for a Private in the Army to receive.

Roy Cohn is speaking for Roy Cohn to give the facts. I have no counsel.

MCCARTHY

The average American can do very little insofar as digging Communists, espionage agents, out of our government—is concerned. They must depend upon those of us whom they send down here to man the watchtowers of the nation. The thing that the American people can do is to be vigilant day and night to make sure they don't have Communists teaching the sons and daughters of America. Now, I realize that the minute anyone tries to get a Communist out of a college, out of a university, there'll be raised the phony cry that you're interfering with academic freedom. I would like to emphasize that there is no academic freedom where a Communist is concerned. He is not a free agent. He has no freedom of thought, no freedom of expression. He must take his orders from Moscow, or he will no longer be a member of the Communist Party. I may say, Mr. Jenkins, I don't care how much of a screwball or a crackpot any professor or teacher may be as long as he or she is a free agent. But once, once you have this United States, from the Atlantic to the Pacific, covered with a network, a network of professors and teachers who are getting their orders from Moscow, from an organization that wants to destroy this nation, that wants to corrupt the minds of youth, then, Mr. Jenkins, we're rapidly losing the battle. The thing that I think we must remember is that this is a war which a brutalitarian force has won to a greater extent than any brutalitarian force has won a war in the history of the world before. For example, uh, Christianity, which has been in existence for two thousand years has not converted, convinced nearly as many people as this Communist brutalitarianism has enslaved in 106 years—and they're not going to stop. I know that many of my good friends seem, uh, to feel this is sort of a game you can play. Uh, that you can talk about Communism as though it's, uh, something, uh, 10,000 miles away. Mr. Jenkins, in answer to your question, let me say it's right here with us now. If we, unless we make sure there's no infiltration of our government, then just as certain as you sit there in the period of our lives, you will see a Red World. Mr. Jenkins, anyone who has followed the Communist conspiracy even remotely, and who can add two and two, will tell you that there is no remote possibility of this war which we're in today, and it's a war, a war which we've been losing—no remote possibility of this ending except by victory or by death for this civilization.

MUNDT

The Committee will please come to order. [*Gavel.*]

SYMINGTON

I suggest that in the interest of these Hearings, the charges are often forgotten. The charges were, did Senator McCarthy and two members of his staff use improper pressure for Mr. David Schine with the Army? The countercharge was that there was blackmail on the part of the Army and the use of Mr. Schine as a hostage. Uh, those are the charges that have been made.

STEVENS

Gentlemen of the Committee: In order that we may all be quite clear as just why this hearing has come about, it is necessary for me to refer at the outset, to Private D., G. David Schine, a former consultant to this Committee. I have been informed, one, from mid-July of last year until March first of this year, David Schine was discussed between one branch or other of the Department of the Army and Senator McCarthy or members of his staff in more than sixty-five telephone calls. Two, this matter was discussed at approximately nineteen meetings between Army personnel and Senator McCarthy or members of his staff. Three, requests made on Schine's behalf ranged from several for a direct commission before he was inducted into the Army to many for special assignments, relief from routine duty such as K.P., extra time off, and special visitor privileges. I may say that during my tenure as Secretary of the Army, there is no record that matches this persistent, tireless effort to obtain special consideration and privileges for this man. The Schine case is only an example of the wrongful seeking of privilege, of the perversion of power—it has been a distraction that has kept many men from the performance of tasks far more important to the welfare of this country than the convenience of a single army private.

ADAMS

I said, let's talk about Schine. And that started a chain of events that, aah, an experience similar to none which I have had in my life. Aah, Mr. Cohn became extremely agitated, and uh, uh, became extremely abusive. The thing that he was so violent about was the fact that the Army was not, uh, was not agreeing to an assignment for Schine. I said to Cohn that I'd like to give him some advice. I pointed out to him that the national interest required that Schine be treated just like every other soldier. Uh—

JENKINS

Well, what was his reply to that, Mr. Adams?

ADAMS

He exploded at that, and he said that if the national interest was the thing we were interested in, he'd give us a little bit. I knew that, ah, 90 per cent of all inductees ultimately face overseas duty, and I knew that one day we were going to face that problem with Mr. Cohn as to Schine. I asked him what would happen if Schine got overseas duty.

JENKINS

You mean you were breaking the news gently, Mr. Adams?

ADAMS

Yes sir, that's right. I asked him what would happen if Schine got overseas duty, and he responded with vigor and force, "Stevens is through as Secretary of the Army." I said, "Oh, Roy," something to this effect, "Oh, Roy, now don't say that." I said, "Come on. Really, what is going to happen if Schine gets overseas duty?" And he responded with even more force, *"We'll wreck the Army."* This was the subject, uh—Schine.

JENKINS

Well, now, do we get it that you deny, you affirm it, or you say you've got no recollection of it? Now let's get it straight.

COHN

I'm telling you, sir. Uhh—number one, I have a pretty good recollection. Number two, I remember that day. Number three, I do not remember saying any of those things, the way Mr. Adams has them. And number four, I checked with the only other person who was there on that occasion, and he says my recollection is correct that I did not make those statements.

JENKINS

And as I get it now, you're saying that you have no recollection of it?

COHN

No, sir. I say I do not recall having said that.

JENKINS

Well, that's, that's what, that's what you're anxious for your answer to be—now you don't recall having said it?

COHN

No, sir.

JENKINS

But you don't deny it?

COHN

Sir, I'm saying I'm sure I did not say it. I am sure—

JENKINS

All right, now you're saying you did not say it, Mr. Cohn.

COHN

Yes, sir. I say I am sure I did not make that statement, and I am sure that Mr. Adams and anybody else with any sense, and Mr. Adams has a lot of sense, could not ever believe that I was threatening to wreck the Army, or that I could wreck the Army. I say, sir, the statement is ridiculous.

JENKINS

I'm talking about Stevens being through as Secretary of the Army.

COHN

That's equally ridiculous, sir.

JENKINS

And untrue.

COHN

Yes, sir. Equally ridiculous and untrue.

STEVENS

Senator McCarthy said that one of the few things that he had trouble with Mr. Cohn about was David Schine. He said that Roy thinks that Dave ought to be a General and operate from a penthouse on the Waldorf Astoria, or words to that effect.

SMITH

"Mr. Cohn telephoned me on the afternoon of July 31st. He stated that Mr. David Schine of the Committee staff was about to be drafted, and that he, Mr. Cohn, and Senator McCarthy felt that he should have a direct commission for which they considered him qualified by education. I phoned General Hull about 4:30 on July 31st. He informed me that Mr. Schine's qualifications did not justify his direct commissioning in any of these branches. General Hull said that the opportunity to qualify for officer candidate training was open to Mr. Schine, as it was to any other citizen drafted into the Armed Forces, and that the Secretary of the Army who was aware of all the facts in the case had directed that the treatment accorded and the opportunities afforded Mr. Schine after his entry into the military service should be the same as for any other American citizen, no more and no less.

"Mr. Cohn came to my office at 11:20 A.M. on August 1st, 1953. I told him the substance of General Hull's reply to my inquiries. I asked if Mr. Schine had had ROTC. Mr. Cohn replied that Mr. Schine had had no ROTC training, and that there appeared to be no chance of a commission in one of the other branches, except at the expense of a protracted term of service. Mr. Cohn then asked if the CIA could not arrange to have Mr. Schine commissioned, as he had investigative experience. I replied that the CIA drew a few commissioned personnel by detail from the Armed Services, but gave them additional training and required a longer tour of duty. However, I offered to telephone Mr. Allen Dulles, director of Central Intelligence, to ask about the possibilities. Mr. Cohn said that I need not do this. The CIA, he said, was too juicy a subject for future investigation, and it would not be right to ask them to get Mr. Schine commissioned and then investigate the organization later.

"Very sincerely, Walter B. Smith."

JENKINS

State whether or not on either of those occasions you felt that Mr. Cohn was being too persistent or was trying to high-pressure anyone—

SMITH

Not me, sir.

JENKINS

Now, Mr. Secretary, that was not a part of your pattern to hold this boy Schine as a sort of a hostage and use him as a bait for the purpose of evading this investigation, was it?

STEVENS

Certainly not. And if he was a hostage so have hundreds of thousands, if not millions, of young Americans been hostages when they were doing their duty in service for their country.

MCCLELLAN

The implication is here—and you just well face it, sir. The implication is here that you were trying to buy off this Committee from investigating the Army. Now, if that is true, you did have the authority to grant the commission and order it granted, didn't you?

STEVENS

Yes, sir.

McCLELLAN

You refused to go that far?

STEVENS

I certainly did.

McCARTHY

Mr. Chairman, a point of order.

MUNDT

The Senator's time has expired. I'll listen to the point of order.

McCARTHY

Mr. Chairman, I want to point out that I think that question is completely improper and unfair. The implication is that this chairman could have been bought off. All the evidence is that this chairman could, under no circumstances, have been bought off this investigation.

JENKINS

Now, Mr., umm, Adams, a charge has been made against you that you not only offered special dispensations for Schine in order to pacify the staff, but that you offered up bigger bait from time to time—to wit, subversives, homosexuals in the Air Force and in the Navy. Did you ever do that, Mr. Adams?

ADAMS

I did not.

JENKINS

We got a definite answer on that, didn't we?

ADAMS

That is correct, sir. You will always get a definite answer on that.

JENKINS

You remember that distinctly?

ADAMS

I remember that distinctly, sir. I never made such an offer, I never would make such an offer. There was under investigation in the Army at that time, and under the supervision of my office being investigated for the Secretary of the Army, some very serious allegations with referenec to homosexual behavior on the part of a group of Army officers at a large Army base in the South. The thing that further—

JENKINS

Well it wasn't in Tennessee, Mr. Adams.

ADAMS

No, sir, it was not. [*Laughter.*]

McCLELLAN

Point of order, point of order, let's exclude Arkansas too.

ADAMS

I can do that, sir.

MUNDT

The Chair would like to raise a point of order on behalf of South Dakota—might also be considered the South.

ADAMS

I can exclude all of the states of the members of this Committee.

JENKINS

Did it come to your attention that this Private David Schine was hiring his fellow soldiers and paying them money to clean his rifle? [*McCarthy laughs.*]

STEVENS

[*Laughs.*] I think I heard something about that later.

JENKINS

Did it come to your attention that he was not cleaning up his quarters, such as other soldiers were required to do according to regulations?

STEVENS

Not while he was at Fort Dix, but I heard about it afterwards.

JENKINS

Heard about it afterwards?

STEVENS

Yes, sir.

JENKINS

Did you know that when the soldiers at Fort Dix were transported from one point in the area to another, to bivouac, and other parts, that Private Schine almost invariably rode in the cab of the truck, whereas the other soldiers, sometimes numbering forty and fifty, were packed like cattle or sheep in the back of the truck and exposed to the weather. Did you learn that?

STEVENS

No, sir.

MCCARTHY

When Counsel says, have you learned that as many as forty young men were packed in the back end of a truck like cattle, that, that is not a hypothetical question? That's completely unfair to the Army. I don't think—I've been in the military for awhile, I've never seen young men treated like cattle. [*Laughter.*] I don't think we should let it go to the mothers of this country that their sons are being treated like cattle, because they are not. It is true that one of the charges made against Mr. Schine, and again may I say that I have no record of this because Mr. Schine has been ordered not to discuss the charges. The only record I have is a left wing paper, who got the charges which we couldn't get—one of the charges was he had his shoes commercially polished. That one of the bits of special favor he got? He was allowed to pay ten cents to have his shoes polished?

STEVENS

I don't know sir.

MCCARTHY

Another charge as announced is that, uh, he had special boots with straps and buckles on the side. In other words, I understand that Dave has about a size 12 or 13 foot, he couldn't get a, he couldn't get a shoe at the usual place so he went downtown and bought a shoe. That's one of the charges against him—You don't think the Committee intervened to allow him to buy a special shoe, do you?

STEVENS

I wouldn't know, I don't have any information on that, Senator McCarthy.

MCCARTHY

Another of the charges was that he had a fur-lined hood. Pretty serious do you think?

STEVENS

What was that?

MCCARTHY

That he has a fur-lined hood. Another that he complained about the cold weather. Do you think this Committee intervened to allow him to complain about the cold weather?

STEVENS

I wouldn't think so, I don't know anything about it.

MCCARTHY

Another charge was that he could've walked in behind a jeep that was parked, he walked in front of the jeep. Do you think that anyone on the Committee called and asked permission for him to walk in front of the jeep?

McCARTHY

Now can't you and I both agree, Colonel, that the average person, back in this audience even, looking at this—the television audience, and they are the jury in this case—can't help but get a completely false impression from these phony charts—and that this is completely dishonest, Colonel. Isn't that true?

BLOUNT

No, sir, it is not true.

McCARTHY

Well can you tell me why they didn't black out the passes, the absences of the average trainee? Why do they only use the symbol to black out Schine—and prepare these huge charts for the television audience?

MCCARTHY

General, would you come over here so I can show you this?

RYAN

I have a copy of it here.

MCCARTHY

Now this was not put out by the Army, General, as far as I know. Was it?

RYAN

Yes, sir, I think it was.

MCCARTHY

Do you know who put it out?

RYAN

I suppose that the counsel which represented the Army prepared this from documentary evidence that, ah, was submitted to them.

McCARTHY

All right, now—

RYAN

But the form, Senator, the black, and, and uh, for Private Schine and the white for the normal trainee, I don't know why the differentiation was made—

McCARTHY

I, I maybe I can—

RYAN

They could have been made both black.

McCARTHY

Maybe I can tell you why, General. It's a dishonest, phony

attempt to deceive the people watching on television, putting up this chart showing everything black on Schine's chart, and showing it white on the average trainee's. Let's black it in. [*The chart is blacked in.*] Just to make sure we're making no mistake you, you'll find that, in all these areas, which we've now blacked in, which were white, Private Schine got a black block for doing exactly the same as the other privates under your command, there isn't that correct?

RYAN

Yes, sir.

MCCARTHY

Good. Now, will you agree with me that that makes this a completely dishonest and a phony chart?

RYAN

No, no, sir, I don't think anything that was put out from the Army is dishonest.

MCCARTHY

General, I think I represent the Army as much as anyone in this room does. I believe that you and I, just in common honesty, would agree that if Schine got a weekend off, it's blacked out, then if another draftee got a weekend off, they should black that, too, wouldn't they? Because after all, this is being tried before an audience, a jury I should say, of quite a few million people.

OFFICER

Sir, all I can give you is my own opinion, and in my opinion, the reason that it was done was just, er, for comparative purposes, just like in a prizefight on television—one of the fighters wears dark trunks, and one of the fighters wears, uh, light trunks. That's the only reason that I can see. [*Laughter.*]

MUNDT

Don't you really feel it would've been more informative and less deceptive to the Committee, when you're preparing charts to be compared, if you had used comparable symbols? Instead of two sets of symbols such as you did use?

BLOUNT

Well, I didn't know that anyone would be deceived by it.

MUNDT

I'm sure your answer was not responsive. It would've avoided all the necessity of calling you in and having this comparison. We would've understood it right from the very beginning, wouldn't we?

BLOUNT

Yes, and I, ah, think it would've been more informative, but so far as deceptive, I had not felt that it had deceived.

MUNDT

I'm not accusing you of attempting to deceive—very frankly you did deceive me.

STEVENS

Mr. Carr called on me with Mr. Roy Cohn on October 2nd, 1953. When they were in my office that day, I considered that they were there for a common purpose, and that Mr. Cohn's statements on behalf of Mr. Schine met with Mr. Carr's approval. Secondly, Mr. Cohn did most of the talking as the chronology indicates. But Mr. Carr, in my recollection also, in a lesser way, a far lesser way, uh, brought up the same thing. As I have said before, Mr. Cohn did most of the talking on this occasion as well as on others, but at no time during the conversation did Mr. Carr take exception to Mr. Cohn's action, or in any way attempt to disassociate himself from the subject of a special assignment for Mr. Schine. The very fact that he was the executive director of the Subcommittee staff and did not object, when I was asked for the convenience of his Subcommittee to make a special assignment for one of his subordinates, left me with a definite impression that he fully concurred in Mr. Cohn's position.

MCCARTHY

Mr. Chairman.

MUNDT

Point of order?

MCCARTHY

Is this a new theory of guilt by silence I wonder?

MUNDT

That is a proper question for the Senator to ask in his own time. I would appreciate it if no spurious, to quote the illustrious counsel, points of order will be made to interrupt the interrogatory which I'm endeavoring to engage.

MCCARTHY

Mr. Chairman.

MUNDT

Point of order overruled.

MCCARTHY

I can assure you there'll be no interruptions, unless I think it's of importance. I do think it's important now to make a point of order that the Secretary is trying to impute guilt by silence to Mr. Carr.

Secretary Stevens, I've been trying to follow your answers both to Senator Mundt and to other Senators, and to Senator Cohn, uh, Mr. Cohn who has asked you about this, uh—you say that Carr backed up Mr. Cohn? Do I understand that you mean he backed him up by silence? Or backed him up by conversation? If he backed him up by conversation, then let's have the conversation.

STEVENS

Well, he, ah, first of all, he did nothing to stop the conversation.

MCCARTHY

All right, then we have silence. You say that he tried to improperly influence. Now if he said something that was improper, we should know what he said. If he didn't say anything improper, if you can't remember anything improper, then you should tell us. Let me say this—I think you're trying to give us an honest account.

STEVENS

That's right.

McCARTHY

Some of my friends don't agree with that, I may say.

COHN

Ah, I might add myself as one of those, sir.

WELCH

You were being asked, uh, at the question, at the top, almost at the top of the page, that this college graduate, referring to Schine, "Partially filled out an application, a form, for a commission in the Army." "Mr. McCarthy: I don't know the slightest thing about the application he filled out." "Mr. Jenkins:

You don't know one thing about that?" "Senator McCarthy: I never saw it." Senator, I have the application that David Schine filled out and I can show you—

McCARTHY

Don't tell me I notarized it. [*He giggles. Laughter in room.*]

WELCH

Sorry?

McCARTHY

I said, don't tell me I notarized it. [*Giggles.*]

WELCH

No, you merely signed it. [*Cheering laughter in committee room.*]

McCARTHY

Don't, don't you think, actually, Mr. Secretary, that this is all uh, ridiculous in the extreme for this Committee and all of these competent Army officers to be sitting here trying to find out why a private in the Army was successively promoted until he is finally up to the very top position of private. What do you think? [*Giggles.*]

STEVENS

Well, I think you would like to have had him something other than a private.

[*McCarthy chuckles amid much committee room laughter and noise. Mundt tries to restore order.*]

MUNDT

Let's have no manifestations of approval or disapproval.

MCCARTHY

Oh, don't mind me. Let—for the time being—for the time being, for the time being, let's assume that what you say is right. If I wanted him as something other than a private, I was awfully unsuccessful, wasn't I? Isn't that right?

STEVENS

But that wasn't your fault, Senator.

MUNDT

Mr. Welch, a point of order?

WELCH

I don't know what it is but it's a point of something. I have—

MUNDT

A point of order will get stated.

WELCH

My point of order is that Mr. Jenkins yesterday was imposed upon and so was the Secretary of the Army by having a doctored or altered photograph produced in this courtroom as if it were honest.

MUNDT

This is a committee room, Mr. Welch.

WELCH

A committee room—and produced as if it were honest. I have the photograph which was offered yesterday in evidence, and in respect to which Mr. Stevens was not only examined but cross-examined, and I show you now a photograph in respect to which I charge that what was offered in evidence yesterday was an altered, shamefully cut down picture so that somebody could say to Stevens, were you not photographed alone with David Schine when the truth is he was photographed in a group. I would like now to offer the picture that I have in my right hand as the original, undoctored, unaltered piece of evidence.

MCCARTHY

Mr. Chairman, the point of order is that Mr. Welch, under the guise of making a point of order has testified that a picture is doctored. I now have before me—I might say that yesterday is the first time I saw either of these pictures—the picture that was introduced yesterday, the one Mr. Welch puts in today. He makes a completely false statement that this was a group picture. It is not—

JENKINS

The Counsel advises the Chair, may I say—

MCCARTHY

May I finish my point of order?

JENKINS

Counsel advises the Chair that if the Senator is engaged in a statement—

MCCARTHY

Mr. Chairman.

SYMINGTON

Point of order.

MCCARTHY

Mr. Chairman, I am getting rather sick of being interrupted in the middle of a sentence. If I may say—

SYMINGTON

Order, order. Point of order.

MCCARTHY

Oh, be quiet, Mr. Chairman.

SYMINGTON

I haven't the slightest intention of being quiet.

MCCARTHY

Mr. Chairman.

SYMINGTON

The Senator is running this Committee, and you're not running this Committee.

MCCARTHY

May I have the floor?

MUNDT

The Chair, the Chair has the floor—to determine whether or not Senator McCarthy is speaking to a point of order.

MCCARTHY

Mr. Chairman.

MUNDT

State your point of order and then speak to it.

MCCARTHY

Mr. Chairman, may I suggest, I'm getting awfully sick of sitting down here at the end of the table and having whoever wants to, interrupt in the middle of a sentence. Now, Mr. Welch made a statement. I raised a point of order that it was not, not a proper point of order. It was not a proper point of order to be raised, and when Mr., Mr. Welch, under the guise of a point of order, said this was a group picture, I suggested that the Chair make the record clear, that Mr. Welch was not speaking the truth, and that the only, the only change in the—

JENKINS

Mr. Chairman. Mr. Chairman, I'm sorry to interrupt the Senator from Wisconsin. I agree with the Senator from Wisconsin that Mr. Welch did not make a point of order. I further make the statement that the Senator from Wisconsin is not making a point of order. I think that should be made perfectly clear to both Mr. Welch and Senator McCarthy.

JENKINS

I ask you whether or not you told me that you had documentary evidence in the form of a photograph of Mr. Stevens and Mr. Schine corroborating your statement to me that Mr. Stevens requested his photograph to be taken with Schine? Is that correct?

COHN

I told you, sir, that we had, that as far as I knew, there was a picture of Mr. Stevens and Private Schine taken on November 17th. There was and there is.

JENKINS

Was that original the photograph introduced yesterday, delivered to me by you or a member of your staff, prior to my cross-examination of the Secretary?

COHN

May I describe it?

JENKINS

Was anything ever said to me up to this time, about any person being cut out of that photograph?

COHN

No, sir, I don't think anything was ever said to you about any person being cut out of that photograph. I now find an inquiry of a member of the staff that they saw some third person, who was not recognizable and was not recognized, standing to the side, but Mr. Stevens and Mr. Schine were facing each other and looking at each other. There was a third person, standing to the side, and they thought that person had no relevancy and had nothing to do with it, and that the picture wanted was the picture of Stevens and Schine.

JULIANA

It was my understanding that a picture of Schine and Secretary

Stevens was to be delivered to you on Friday morning.

JENKINS

Did I say anything about cutting out of a picture any individual, mister?

JULIANA

No, sir.

JACKSON

You, you don't think the picture was changed?

JULIANA

No, sir.

JACKSON

Well, what's your definition of change?

JULIANA

If you will take Mr. Stevens and Mr. Schine in the large, blown-up portion, I think you will find that they are the same as these individuals.

JACKSON

There is nothing else different in the picture?

JULIANA

Sure, this individual here has been left off.

JACKSON

So that's not a change.

JULIANA

I don't think there's any change in these two individuals, no.

JACKSON

Well, I don't think there's been any testimony by anyone in this proceeding that there was a change made of the photographic appearance of the Secretary of the Army and Mr. Schine. Has there been?

JULIANA

I, I couldn't answer that, sir.

JACKSON

Well, I mean, do you know if there's been any change? The two pictures are there in front of you.

JULIANA

I, I don't—I'm no photographer, but I don't think there's been a change.

McCARTHY

Mr. Chairman.

MUNDT

Do you have a point of order?

McCARTHY

Yes, I certainly have. Uh, Mr. Chairman, my point of order is this: that Mr. Jackson talked about a picture that had been changed, and after he had made the statement, he starts questioning the witness about his own statements. I think it's unfair to the witness—oh, drop it.

WELCH

Well, then, the only thing to do is to bring in the photostat of the original picture with three people in the cast, isn't that right?

JULIANA

I wasn't asked for it, and I didn't deliver it.

WELCH

I think that's right. You were asked for something different from the thing that hung on Schine's wall.

JULIANA

I never knew what hung on Schine's wall.

WELCH

You did know what hung on Schine's wall when that was handed to you, sir.

JULIANA

I did not know what hung on Schine's wall.

WELCH

Did you think this came from a pixie? [*Laughter.*] Where did you think this picture that I hold in my hand came from?

JULIANA

I have no idea where it came from.

MCCARTHY

Will that question be reread?

MUNDT

It will be reread.

REPORTER

Question: Did you think this came from a pixie?

MCCARTHY

Would Counsel, for my benefit, define—I think he might be an expert on this—the word "pixie"?

WELCH

I should say, I should say, Mr. Senator, that a pixie is a close relative of a fairy. [*Laughter.*] Shall I proceed sir? Have I enlightened you?

MCCARTHY

As I said, as I said, I think you might be an authority on what a pixie is.

MUNDT

Counsel may proceed.

WELCH

Although I sit at the same table, I'm not your counsel. [*Laughter.*]

COHN

There is not a statement that's been made at this hearing with which I'm in more complete agreement, Mr. Welch, although I say, I am sure you're a lawyer of great ability, and maybe I would be fortunate if I had you as my counsel. I have no counsel. Roy Cohn is here speaking for Roy Cohn to give the facts. I have no counsel, and I feel the need of none, sir.

WELCH

In all modesty, sir, I am content that it should appear from my end that I am not your counsel.

COHN

I must say, you're certainly not going to get any fee from me, Mr. Welch.

WELCH

Mr. Cohn, you have spoken of that picture as representing Mr. Stevens smiling at Schine. Do you look at it now with me? [*Laughter.*]

COHN

Let, let's have the photo right up here.

WELCH

That's good enough.

COHN

Let's see if we can look at it closer.

WELCH

Well, let's have it there. That's good enough.

COHN

Mr. Welch, may I confess to slight case of nearsightedness here and I, I hope that's not nearsightedness in connection with my duties, but it is when it comes to—excuse me, I'd like to have that right up here—

WELCH

I think you have betrayed some nearsightedness. Have it as close as you would like. [*Laughter.*]

COHN

Mr. Welch, I'd like to say here again, I uh, I'd be very glad to answer your questions here. I don't think I'm quite as clever as you are, and I'm afraid I'm not going to be able to answer your quips.

WELCH

Oh, Mr. Cohn. [*Nodding to Cohn.*] My question, now, is this. You have referred to that picture as showing Mr. Secretary Stevens smiling at Dave Schine. Are you now close enough to the picture so that you would like to qualify that statement?

COHN

Sir, I would accept your characterization of the picture.

WELCH

It's a grim smile on Steven's face.

COHN

I accept it. If you want to call Mr. Stevens' smile a grim smile, sir, I fully accept what you say. To me it's a picture of Secretary Stevens. If it's a grim smile, so be it. It's a picture of Private Schine; they're standing next to each other, they are facing each other. Their eyes are meeting, they are looking at each other, and if the smile is grim, or it isn't grim, uh, I know not, sir.

WELCH

Not too fast, Mr. Cohn. Not too fast. Mr. Stevens is looking to his right. Isn't he?

COHN

Well, sir, my—

WELCH

Isn't he? Just look at it, you can answer that one easily.

COHN

Mr. Welch, do you want to imply that I'm not answering it? You asked me a question and then you say it with the implication as though I can't answer it.

WELCH

Well, answer it. Mr. Stevens is looking to his right, isn't he?

COHN

Sir, if you'll give me the chance, I'll try to answer it.

WELCH

By all means, sir.

COHN

Thank you. Uh, I, the picture to me, looks as though Mr. Stevens and Private Schine are looking at each other.

WELCH

My question was a simple one. Mr. Stevens is looking to his right, is he not?

COHN

Yes, I would say he is probably looking to his right, and Private Schine is standing to his right.

WELCH

And on Mr. Stevens' right are two figures. Is that correct?

COHN

Yes, that's correct. On Mr. Stevens' right there are two figures.

WELCH

And one is Private Schine.

COHN

Yes, sir.

WELCH

And further to Mr. Stevens' right is Colonel Bradley.

COHN

Standing sideways.

WELCH

It would take someone with clairvoyance to know to whom Secretary Stevens is looking, would it not?

COHN

No, sir, I don't think so. It would take somebody with common sense who can look at a picture and see what's in it.

WELCH

I think I observe on Colonel Bradley's face a faint little look of pleasure. Do you, sir?

COHN

I would say—[*Laughing.*]—I know that Colonel Bradley had a good steak dinner shortly after this. Maybe he was anticipating it. I do know that Colonel Bradley looks to me as though he is looking at Private Schine.

WELCH

Well, now, if Bradley is feeling good about a steak dinner, Schine must be considering a whole haunch of beef, is he not? [*Laughter.*]

MCCARTHY

How long, Mr. Chairman—Mr. Chairman.

MUNDT

Do you have a point of order?

MCCARTHY

Yes, it's a point of order. How long must we put up with this circus? If the Counsel, the Counsel is trying to elicit information, good. If he's looking for a laugh from an audience, then don't talk about any physical defects of my chief counsel. It's so, so indecent, so dishonest. I'm not talking about any physical defects that Counsel Welch may have. I do not intend to. Let's get down to the issues, Mr. Welch. Each minute, Mr. Chairman, may I point out, each minute we waste here is wasting a vast amount of manpower, very important manpower I think. The manpower of eight senators and the heads of our military establishment.

SYMINGTON

In these proceedings, to the best of my knowledge, for the first time in our history, our people have been urged to entertain serious doubts as to the dedication and loyalty of our armed forces from top to bottom.

ADAMS

This is a letter signed Dwight D. Eisenhowever, addressed to the Honorable Secretary of Defense, Washington, D. C.: "Dear Mr. Secretary: It is essential to the successful working of our system that the persons intrusted with power in any one of the three great branches of government shall not encroach upon the authority confided to the others. The ultimate responsibility for the conduct of the executive branch rests with the President.

"However, throughout our history, the President has withheld information whenever he found that what was sought was confidential or its disclosure would be incompatible with the public interest, or jeopardize the safety of the nation. Because it is essential to efficient and effective administration that employees of the executive branch be in a position to be completely candid in advising with each other on official matters, and because it is not in the public interest that any of their conversations or communications or any documents or reproductions concerning such advice be disclosed, you will instruct employees of your department that in all of their appearances before the Subcommittee of the Senate Committee on Government Operations regarding the inquiry now before it, they are not to testify to any such conversations or communications or to produce any such documents or reproductions.

"I direct this action so as to maintain the proper separation of powers between the executive and legislative branches of the government in accordance with my responsibilities and duties under the Constitution. This separation is vital to preclude the exercise of arbitrary power by any branch of the government.

"Sincerely, Dwight D. Eisenhower."

MUNDT

Thank you. The Chair will recognize Senator McCarthy or Mr. Cohn.

MCCARTHY

Mr. Chairman, I, must admit that I'm somewhat at a loss as to know how to—what to do at this moment. One of the subjects of this inquiry is to find out who was responsible for succeeding in calling off the hearing of Communist infiltration in government. At this point I find out there's no way of ever getting at the truth. The iron curtain is pulled down so we can't tell what happened. There's no reason why anyone should be afraid of the facts. The question is, how far, how far can, I'm not talking about the present occupant of the White House, but we got a tremendously important question here, Mr. Chairman. That is, how far can the President go? Uh, who all can he order not to testify? Then any president, we don't know who will be president, 1956, 1960, 1964, any president—[*Committee room laughter, McCarthy chuckles.*] I won't repeat that. [*McCarthy chuckles again.*] Any president can, by an executive order, keep the facts from the American people, and as I say, I think that—I don't believe that this is the result of President Eisenhower's own personal thinking. I am sure if he knew what this was all about, that he would not sign an order saying that you cannot tell the Senate Committee what went on when they cooked up those charges against Mr. Cohn, Mr. Carr, and myself.

Someone for his own benefit should contact the President immediately and point out to him perhaps, that he and I and many of us campaigned and promised the American people we would no longer involve, engage in government by secrecy, white-wash, and cover up; and I think that these facts should be brought to the President because the American people will not stand for this.

Let's go through, let's lay all the facts upon the table, and we can't lay the facts upon the table if we're going to draw an iron curtain—and we're half way through the hearings, so, Mr. Chairman, I would like to ask for an executive session, a meeting in the Committee so I will know to what extent the Committee is going to honor this order or any other order like it. May I say, Mr. Chairman, I feel that the Senate must determine that we're entitled to all of this information, and what Mr. Jenkins says here as Counsel, what you say as Chairman can be quoted as precedent in the future when we decide just how far the President can go in a secrecy order. May I say that I think if the witness asserts a type of Fifth Amendment privilege here—

ADAMS

I'm not asserting Fifth Amendment privilege, Senator—

McCARTHY

Uh—some presidential privilege—I think the Chair should allow him to do it rather than to get into this, uh, question which will take us months to decide. Ultimately, may I finish, Mr. Chairman, I think this is infinitely more important than anything we bring out at this hearing. It's a question of just what a President can do. Now I disagree as the Chair knows with the Truman blackout order of 1948. I think that Eisenhower had been badly advised. I think there's only one person can claim a privilege, whether it's a Fifth Amendment privilege, whether it's a presidential privilege, or any other—

ADAMS

Mr. Chairman, just a moment, sir . . .

McCARTHY

May I—may I finish—

ADAMS

I don't like the Senator from Wisconsin inferring that I'm claiming the Fifth Amendment privilege because I'm not, and I'm not claiming any privilege on this memorandum. This is an instruction from the President of the United States and I consider myself bound by it, sir.

McCARTHY

Mr. Chairman, Mr. Chairman, may I say that I think it's very important that we follow the time-worn rule of law, that no one can exert a privilege except the witness. I don't care whether it's a Fifth Amendment privilege, whether it's this new privilege that we have today, or what it is.

McCARTHY

Mr. Stevens, I am getting awfully weary of this attempt to get a few simple facts from you as though we're pulling teeth. We've spent just a vast amount of time here trying to get answers to some simple questions.
The question is this. You made a statement this morning under oath. You say, "I wish to make it perfectly plain that the decisions and the acts on the part of the Army concerning the controversy presently being heard by the Senate Subcommittee were the decisions and the acts of the Department of the Army alone." Now do you still stand by that statement?

STEVENS

I do.

MCCARTHY

Do you say that John Adams was not telling the truth when he said that the decision was made in the Justice Department, with White House aides present, with the Attorney General present, the Deputy Attorney present, the Ambassador to the U. N. present. Now I'm sure that any man who can add two and two, Mr. Secretary, will agree that that completely contradicts your statement that all decisions were the decisions of the Department of the Army alone. I wonder if you want your, your sworn testimony this morning to stand as it is or not?

STEVENS

I want it to stand.

MCCARTHY

Mr. Secretary, here is the testimony of Mr. Browder, and I take this from a report, dated, eh, let's see. Just a minute—

STEVENS

Does that mean I am a Communist, Senator?

MCCARTHY

That's awfully funny, isn't it, Mr. Secretary? That's terribly funny. I've made it very clear to you at all times that I felt that you are anti-Communist. I've also made it very clear to you that I thought that you were very naïvely and unintelligently anti-Communist. You know that, Mr. Secretary?

JACKSON

I'm a little confused here. This is a copy of a letter that's being introduced, and I'd like to know how it arrived here at the Committee. Where it came from? How did it get here?

JENKINS

It was handed to me just now, by Senator McCarthy. It purports to be a letter written October 26th, 1951, to the Federal Bureau of Investigation and signed by J. Edgar Hoover, the Director. It is addressed to Major General Boling, Assistant Chief of Staff, G2, Department of the Army, Washington, D.C.

JACKSON

Well, I understand that it could readily be identified whether this was a matter that was subpoenaed from the Army files or whether the Army voluntarily gave it to—

WELCH

Mr. Chairman.

MUNDT

Mr. Welch.

WELCH

I respectfully suggest that that be done. I am a lawyer, and, uh, the appearance of what purports to be a copy of a letter from J. Edgar Hoover in 1951 addressed to some Colonel, is that right sir?

JENKINS

Major General.

WELCH

Major General. The mere fact that we have an impressive looking, purported copy of such a letter doesn't impress an old-time lawyer. I would like to have Mr. J. Edgar Hoover say that he wrote the letter and mailed it. Then we'd know what we're dealing with.

MCCARTHY

Mr. Chairman.

MUNDT

Senator McCarthy.

MCCARTHY

The original, uh—I want to question the Secretary as to whether or not the original of this and other letters like it are in the file. I want to make it very clear that I have gotten neither this letter or anything else from the FBI.

WELCH

Well, where did it come from then? Mr. Chairman, I—I assure you the—this purported copy did not come from the Army files nor did the Senator for a moment suggest it did.

MCCARTHY

Just—just a minute. Now, let me see.

MUNDT

Mr. McCarthy.

MCCARTHY

Now, Mr. Chairman, if Mr. Welch is going to say there's not a copy of this in the Army files, he should be sworn because that statement is untrue as far as I know.

WELCH

I did not say that, Senator. I said that this purported copy did not come from the Army files, and you know I'm quite right sir, and I have an absorbing curiosity to know how in the dickens you got hold of it. [*Laughter.*]

MCCARTHY

I will, I will read—may I say, Mr. Chair—

MUNDT

The Chair has the floor.

MCCARTHY

May I say, Mr. Chair—

MUNDT

The Chair has the floor. I'll have to advise you again, Mr. Welch, that all investigative agencies in this town operate on the rule that they don't have to disclose the source of their information. Your absorbing curiosity will have to be satisfied some other way, I'm afraid.

WELCH

And by Mr. J. Edgar Hoover.

McCARTHY

Can I cut in here?

MUNDT

Senator McCarthy.

McCARTHY

I'd just like to question Mr. Stevens. Mr. Stevens, would you look at that letter, and tell us, number one, whether or not you've ever seen it or were ever notified of its contents?

STEVENS

I'd like to—if I'm—

McCARTHY

I think you should read the letter.

STEVENS

I'd like to have the advice of counsel if I may as to whether or not I'm at liberty to discuss a letter from Mr. J. Edgar Hoover. [*Letter is passed to Stevens.*]

McCARTHY

You're at liberty to read it.

STEVENS

I think it's very bad policy to discuss this thing without Mr. Hoover's knowing about it. [*Welch glances over the letter.*]

McCARTHY

Would you like to read it first?

WELCH

And, may I add, Mr. Chairman, I have the letter in my hand and it's headed "Personal and Confidential, Via Liaison," which seem to be to be rather severe words of a confidential nature. I think Mr. Stevens is quite right in saying that this is a matter that ought to be released by J. Edgar Hoover before we deal with it in this room.

COLLIER

"Mr. Hoover has examined the document and has advised me

that he never wrote any such letter. And because the documents constitutes an unauthorized use of information which is classified as confidential, it is my opinion that is should not be made public. Sincerely yours, Herbert Brownell, Jr., Attorney General."

WELCH

Now, Mr. Collier, as I understand your testimony, this document that I hold in my hand is a carbon copy of precisely nothing. Is that right?

COLLIER

I will say that Mr. Hoover informed me that it is not a carbon copy of a memorandum prepared or sent by the FBI.

WELCH

Let's have it straight from the shoulder. So far as you know, it's a carbon copy of precisely nothing?

COLLIER

So far as I know, it is, yes. But that, again, is a—

WELCH

And so far as you know, this document in this courtroom sprung yesterday by Senator McCarthy is a perfect phony. Is that right?

COLLIER

No sir. I, uh—uh, that is your conclusion. I will not uphold such a conclusion.

WELCH

Well, you've just told us that it's—

MCCARTHY

Mr. Chairman.

MUNDT

Would you care to make a point of order?

MCCARTHY

Yes, Mr. Chairman. I think that, uh, the Chair should insist upon certain rules of honesty on the part of the Counsel for Mr. Stevens, Mr. Adams. Mr. Chairman, this has been referred to as a phony by Mr. Welch. That's one of the most serious reflections upon the integrity of the Chairman that we've had so far, and I've had many reflections upon my integrity.

MUNDT

The Chair has not read the letter, and Mr. Welch has not read the letter, so I suppose we labor under some difficulties.

WELCH

We do. I have higher standards as to my own conduct in respect to these documents than the Senator and his staff have. I do not think it is proper for Mr. Collier to read it and he had declined to read it. I do not think it would be proper for Welch to read it and he has declined to read it, and I await with much interest the Senator's explanation of how it reached his hands and when he read it.

JENKINS

Now, Senator McCarthy, you are bound to be aware of the fact that some attack has been made upon that letter.

MCCARTHY

Just let me make it very clear, Mr. Jenkins and Mr. Chairman, that I will not under any circumstances reveal the source of any information which I get as Chairman of the Committee. Now, one of the reasons that I have been successful, I believe to some extent in exposing the, uh—Communism is because the people who give me information from within the government know that their confidence will not be violated. There is no way on earth that any committee, any force can get me to violate the confidence of those people.

JENKINS

Then, Senator, you did not get the two-and-a-quarter-page document from the Federal Bureau of Investigation?

McCARTHY

I did not, sir.

JENKINS

Now I'm not going to ask you and I did not intend to ask you the name of the individual who gave you that document. But, as I do understand it, Senator McCarthy, and we are trying to pursue this question to its logical end so that the Committee may know all of the facts, that two-and-a-quarter-page document was delivered to you by someone from the Army.

McCARTHY

Yes, I can go a step further, Mr. Jenkins, and—

JENKINS

And perhaps in the Intelligence Department, can you go that far?

McCARTHY

An officer in the Intelligence Department.

WELCH

Senator McCarthy, when you took the stand you, of course, understood you were going to be asked about this letter, did you not?

McCARTHY

I assumed that to be the subject.

WELCH

And you, of course, understood you were going to be asked the source from which you got it.

McCARTHY

I never try to—

WELCH

Ah, just did you understand you would be asked the source?

McCARTHY

No, I will answer that. I never try to read the minds of the senators for what they will ask me.

WELCH

Could I have the oath that you took read to us slowly by the reporter?

MUNDT

Mr. Welch, that doesn't seem to be an appropriate question. You were present. You took the oath yourself. You took the same oath he took.

WELCH

The oath included a promise, a solemn promise by you to tell the truth, comma, the whole truth, comma, and nothing but the truth. Is that correct, sir?

McCARTHY

Mr. Welch, you are not the first individual who tried to get me to betray the confidence and give up the names of my informants. You will be no more successful than those who tried in the past—period.

WELCH

I am only asking you, sir, did you realize when you took that oath, that you were making a solemn promise to tell the whole truth to this Committee?

MCCARTHY

I understand the oath, Mr. Welch.

WELCH

And when you took it, did you have some mental reservations, some Fifth or Sixth Amendment notion that you could measure what you would tell?

MCCARTHY

I don't take the Fifth or Sixth Amendments.

WELCH

Have you some private reservation, when you take the oath that you will tell the whole truth, that lets you be the judge of what you will testify to?

MCCARTHY

The answer is there is no reservation about telling the whole truth.

WELCH

Thank you, sir. Then tell us who delivered the document to you.

MCCARTHY

The answer is no. You will not get that information.

WELCH

You wish then to put your own interpretation on your oath and tell us less than the whole truth?

MCCARTHY

Mr. Welch, I think I made it very clear to you that neither you nor anyone else will ever get me to violate the confidence of loyal people in this government who give me information about Communist infiltration. I repeat, you will not get their names, you will not get any information which will allow you to identify them so that you or anyone else can get their jobs. You can go right ahead and try until doomsday.

SYMINGTON

According to testimony presented this Committee yesterday,

the officer informant who gave this obviously fraudulent letter, was guilty of sending secret information to somebody not authorized to receive it and in so doing, disobeyed the orders of his superiors. In view of the testimony, Mr. Chairman, I do hope that every effort will be made to find out who was the informant. But at least as important should be knowledge on the part of the eight government agencies who sit on the Intelligence Advisory Committee that they may now have in their midst someone who is willing for whatever reason he considers proper to distribute secret information to unauthorized people. Thank you, Mr. Chairman.

MCCLELLAN

I want to say this. I think the position that if the party who takes the document is committing a theft or violating the law, then I doubt that anyone is authorized to receive it.

MCCARTHY

May I make it very clear at the beginning that as far as I'm concerned, the Truman directive, no directive will preclude me from examining material bearing upon the security of this nation. The Senators must, if they are to perform their duty, must see this sequence of letters from the FBI, in which they point out day after day after day what a dangerous situation we have in our top secret radar laboratories, why the tremendous efforts have been made to call this Committee off the investigation, the disclosure of Communists in government.

MUNDT

The Chair is in no position to override the ruling of the Attorney General. He submitted it in writing, and got an answer back in writing and suggests therefore that the Senator continue with his interrogatories in conformity with the Attorney General's opinion.

McCARTHY

Mr. Chairman, does the Chair take the position that a Committee of the Senate, uh, cannot differ with, uh, an appointive officer, the Attorney General? Certainly the Chair doesn't take that position. Mr. Chairman, if the Attorney General has some good reason why these documents should not be made available to the Committee, he should not be bashful about coming down to an Executive Session and telling us why, Mr. Chairman.

McCLELLAN

May I say to you, I am trying to settle a basic issue of law, I don't want any of your confidential information. All I want is to let the country get this legal question settled so we can all operate within the law, if that's possible. I say for myself. You're saying what you'll do and what you'll not do. I tell you, Senator, that I will not set myself up above and apart from the law. I'm going to conform to it. Now you do as you please.

McCARTHY

Will the Senator, will the Senator yield for a minute?

McCLELLAN

Yes.

McCARTHY

May I say, Senator, just for your benefit, I am not setting myself above any law. But, Senator, I just will not abide by any secrecy directive of anyone. I think you and I have and will see Presidents come and go.

McCLELLAN

Senator—

McCARTHY

We have a duty, we have a duty to do our job even though we may differ with a perfectly honest version of what the President thinks his job is.

McCLELLAN

Well, we may differ about that, and that's what I think the American people are entitled to have settled, whether you're right or the President's right. That's what I'm trying to find out. And when you say I'm trying to put you in jail, I'm asking no such thing. I don't care if you stay in or out. No one's afraid of you out anymore than they would be in, as far as I know. But the point I'm making is, Joe, and you know it, we've reached the crossroads in this thing, and we're entitled in the course of these hearings now, to have this thing settled if

there's any way to settle it, and that's all I want.
I don't care, you can keep all your information in your head or somewhere else as far as I'm concerned, now I want you to understand that. I want to settle the basic issue here that is vital, I think, to the security of this nation.

SYMINGTON

Senator McCarthy, do you think that President Eisenhower could put any classification on the secret document which would prevent you from being a person authorized to receive it and examine it?

MCCARTHY

Now, your question was, does Mr. Eisenhower have what?

SYMINGTON

President Eisenhower, sir.

MCCARTHY

President Eisenhower have what? [*Laughter.*]

SYMINGTON

Do you think that President Eisenhower could put any classification on the secret document which could prevent you from being a person authorized to receive and examine it?

MCCARTHY

I guess the answer is yes or no.

JACKSON

My recollection was that in this now famous two-and-a-quarter-page document, there were about thirty-five names listed. This is pretty serious. Have we had anything this serious so far?

McCARTHY

Well, yes, I think we've got something much more serious right now. But, that—

JACKSON

Well, I'm talking about prior to this hearing.

McCARTHY

Let me answer that question now. I think we've got a much more serious situation now in Communist infiltration of the CIA. It disturbs me beyond words.

JACKSON

Well, we haven't, the members of the Committee have not been advised, and I do think that—

McCARTHY

Oh, yes they have. Oh, yes, they have.

JACKSON

Have we, have the names and, of the people . . .

McCARTHY

I discussed this matter with the members of the Committee. I have also discussed with the Committee the question of Communist infiltration of atomic and hydrogen bomb plants. I felt that was, I think, even more important than this infiltration at Monmouth.

JACKSON

May I, may I, just let me finish in view of this one point. May I have from the files all the memos and meetings and minutes with reference to this matter so that we on the Committee can be fully informed.

McCARTHY

You certainly may, Senator, you certainly may.

McCLELLAN

May I ask, Mr. Chairman, have we yet received the names, and I assume they're in the files, of the claimed 133 Communists that are ready for investigation? I've asked for them. Have I yet received them?

McCARTHY

Ah, you would know better than I, Senator. The information is available to you.

MCCLELLAN

I'd like to know something in advance. I'd like to have at least a little advance information.

MCCARTHY

Senator McClellan, may I say that you know that I have been tied up here day and night, with this investigation. I frankly don't have the time now, and that's one of the reasons why I object to this show of continuing on the road. But as soon as we get through this, I'm sure that Senator McClellan knows this, that I have always been completely frank with him. He can have every piece of information we have. It so happens, as you know, I've got a lot of respect for the Senator from Arkansas. I hope—

MCCLELLAN

Thank you.

MCCARTHY

I hope that doesn't hurt you in your campaign.

MCCLELLAN

I think you know I never want anything but what's fair. That's all I'm asking now.

MCCARTHY

You, you will have every piece of information, John, that you—

MCCLELLAN

I'll be very glad to get it. That's what I've requested at your convenience. I hope it'll be soon.

WELCH

Mr. Cohn, what is the exact number of Communists or subversives that are loose today in these defense plants?

COHN

Uh, yes, sir, I'm going to try to particularize for you, if I can.

WELCH

I'm in a hurry. I don't want the sun to go down while they're still in there if we can get them out.

COHN

I'm afraid we won't be able to work that fast.

WELCH

Well, I've got a suggestion about it, sir. How many are there?

COHN

I believe the figure is approximately 130.

WELCH

Approximately one three oh.

COHN

Those are people, Mr. Welch—

WELCH

I don't care. You've told us who they are. And how many plants are there?

COHN

How many plants?

WELCH

How many plants.

COHN

Yes, sir. Just one minute, sir. I see sixteen offhand.

WELCH

Sixteen plants. Are you alarmed at that situation, Mr. Cohn?

COHN

Yes, sir, I am.

WELCH

Nothing could be more alarming, could it?

COHN

It's certainly a very alarming thing.

WELCH

Will you not, before the sun goes down, give those names to the FBI and at least have those men put under surveillance?

COHN

Sir, if there is need for surveillance in case of espionage or anything like that, I can well assure you Mr. John Edgar Hoover and his men know a lot better than I, and I might respectfully suggest, sir, than probably a lot of us, just who should be put under surveillance. I do not purpose to tell the FBI how to run its job.

WELCH

And they do it. And they do it, don't they Mr. Cohn?

COHN

When the need arises, of course.

WELCH

Then they've got the whole 130 have they, Mr. Cohn?

COHN

I am sure of it, sir, and a lot more.

WELCH

Then what's all the excitement about if J. Edgar Hoover is on the job, chasing those 130 Communists.

COHN

Mr. Welch, all the excitement—

WELCH

Well, then, as a second line of defense, let's send the 130 names to the Department of Defense tonight. Would you mind doing that?

COHN

Whatever the Committee directs on that, sir, I will—

WELCH

I wish the Committee would direct that all the names be sent both to the FBI and to the Department of Defense with extreme suddenness.

SYMINGTON

Mr. Chairman, I so move.

MCCARTHY

Mr. Chairman, in view of . . .

MUNDT

Do you have a point of order?

MCCARTHY

Uh—not exactly, Mr. Chairman, but in view of Mr. Welch's request that, uh, the information be given if we know of anyone who might be performing any work for the Communist Party, I think we should tell him that he has in his law firm a young man named Fisher whom he recommended incidentally to do the work on this Committee, who has been, for a number of years, a member of an organization which is named, oh years and years ago, as the legal bulwark for the Communist Party, an organization which always springs to the defense, uh, of anyone who, uh, dares to expose Communists. Uh, I certainly assume that Mr. Welch did not know of this, uh, uh, young man at the time he recommended him as the assistant counsel for this Committee, but he has such terror and such a great desire to know where anyone is located. You may be serving the Communist cause, Mr. Welch, and I thought we should just call to your attention the fact that your Mr. Fisher, who is still in your law firm today, whom you asked to have down here looking over the secret and classified material, is a member of an organization, not named by me, but named by, uh, various committees named by the Attorney General, as I recall. Uh, he belonged to it long after it had been exposed, as the legal arm of the Communist Party. Knowing that, Mr. Welch, I just felt that I had a duty to, uh, respond here to your urgent request that before sundown that if we know of anyone serving the Communist cause we let the agency know. We're now letting you know your man did belong to this organization for either three or four years. Belonged to it long after he was out of law school. And I have hesitated bringing that up, but I have been rather bored with your phony requests to Mr. Cohn here, that he personally get every Communist out of Government before sundown. Therefore, we will give you the information about the young man in your organization. Now, I'm not asking you at this time to explain why you tried to foist him on this Committee. That you did, the Committee knows.

Uh, whether you knew that he was a member of that Communist organization or not, I don't know. I assume you did not, Mr. Welch, because I get the impression that while you are quite an actor, you play for a laugh, I don't think you have any conception of the danger of the Communist Party. I don't think you yourself would ever knowingly aid the Communist cause. I think you're unknowingly siding with it when you try to burlesque this hearing in which we're attempting to bring out the facts.

WELCH

Mr. Chairman.

MUNDT

The Chair may say that he has no recognition or no memory of Mr. Welch recommending either Mr. Fisher or anybody else as counsel for this Committee.

MCCARTHY

I refer to the record, Mr. Chairman on the, to the news story on that.

WELCH

Mr. Chairman. Under the circumstances, I must myself have something approaching a personal privilege.

MUNDT

You may have—

WELCH

Senator McCarthy, I did not know, Senator. Senator, sometimes you say may I have your attention.

MCCARTHY

I'm listening.

WELCH

May I have your attention.

MCCARTHY

I can listen with one ear. [*Laughs.*]

WELCH

Now this time, sir, I want you to listen with both. Senator McCarthy, I think until this moment—

MCCARTHY

Good. Just a minute. Jim, Jim, will you get the news story to the effect that this man belonged to the—to this Communist front organization—

WELCH

I will tell you that he belonged to it.

MCCARTHY

Jim, will you get the citation, one of the citations showing that this was the legal arm of the Communist Party, and the length of time that he belonged, and the fact that he was recommended by Mr. Welch.

WELCH

Senator, you won't need anything in the record when I finish telling you this. Until this moment, Senator, I think I never really gauged your cruelty or your recklessness. Fred Fisher is a young man who went to the Harvard Law School and came into my firm and is starting what looks to be a brilliant career with us. When I decided to work for this Committee, I asked Jim St. Clair, who sits on my right, to be my first assistant. I said to Jim, "Pick somebody in the firm to work under you that you would like." He chose Fred Fisher and they came down on an afternoon plane. That night, when we had taken a little stab at trying to see what the case was about, Fred Fisher and Jim St. Clair and I went to dinner together. I then said to these two young men, "Boys, I don't know anything about you, except I've always liked you, but if there's anything funny in the life of either one of you that would hurt anybody in this case you speak up quick." And Fred Fisher said, "Mr. Welch, when I was in the law school, and for a period of months after, I belonged to the Lawyers' Guild," as you have suggested, Senator.

He went on to say, "I am Secretary of the Young Republican's League in Newton with the son of the Massachusetts governor, and I have the respect and admiration of my community, and I'm sure I have the respect and admiration of the twenty-five lawyers or so in Hale & Dorr." And I said, "Fred, I just don't think I'm going to ask you to work on the case. If I do, one of these days that will come out, and go over national television and it will just hurt like the dickens." And so, Senator, I asked him to go back to Boston. Little did I dream you could be so reckless and so cruel as to do an injury to that lad. It is true, he is still with Hale & Dorr. It is true that he will continue to be with Hale & Dorr. It is, I regret to say, equally true that I fear he shall always bear a scar needlessly inflicted by you. If it were in my power to forgive you for your reckless cruelty, I would do so. I like to think I'm a gentle man, but your forgiveness will have to come from someone other than me.

McCARTHY

Mr. Chairman. Mr. Chairman. May I say that Mr. Welch talks

about this being cruel and reckless. He was just baiting. He has been baiting Mr. Cohn here for hours, requesting that Mr. Cohn before sundown get out of any department of the government anyone who is serving the Communist cause. Now, I just give this man's record and I want to say, Mr. Welch, that it had been labeled long before he became a member, as early as 1944—

WELCH

Senator, may we not drop this? We know he belonged to the Lawyers' Guild. And Mr. Cohn nods his head at me. I did you, I think, no personal injury, Mr. Cohn.

COHN

No, sir.

WELCH

I meant to do you no personal injury, and if I did, I beg your pardon. Let us not assassinate this lad further, Senator. You've done enough. Have you no sense of decency, sir, at long last? Have you left no sense of decency?

McCARTHY

I know this hurts you, Mr. Welch.

WELCH

I'll say it hurts.

McCARTHY

Mr. Chairman, as a point of personal privilege, I'd like to finish this.

WELCH

Senator, I think it hurts you too, sir.

McCARTHY

I'd like to finish this. I know Mr. Cohn would rather not have me go into this. Uh, I intend to, however, and Mr. Welch talks about any sense of decency. It seems that Mr. Welch is pained so deeply he thinks it's improper for me to give the record, the Communist-front record of a man whom he wanted to foist upon this Committee. But it doesn't pain him at all, there's no pain in his chest—about the attempt to destroy the reputation and the, take the jobs away from the young men who are working on my Committee; and Mr. Welch, if, if I have said anything here which is untrue, then tell me. I have heard you and everyone else talk so much about laying the truth upon the table. But when I heard—the completely phony—Mr. Welch, I've been listening now for a long time, saying, now before sundown you must get these people out of government. So I just want you to have it very clear, very clear that you were not so serious about that when you tried to recommend this man for this Committee.

MUNDT

The chair would like to say again that we do not believe Mr. Welch recommended Mr. Fisher as counsel for this Committee; because he has through his office, all the recommendations that had been made, and I do not recall any of them coming from Mr. Welch, and that would include Mr. Fisher.

McCARTHY

Well, let me ask Mr. Welch. You brought him down, did you not? To act as your assistant?

WELCH

Mr. McCarthy, I will not discuss this further with you. You have sat within six feet of me and could ask, could have asked me about Fred Fisher. You have seen fit to bring it out and if there is a God in heaven, it will do neither you nor your cause any good. I will not discuss it further. I will not ask Mr. Cohn any more witnesses. You, Mr. Chairman, may, if you will, call the next witness. [*Applause from committee room.*]

SYMINGTON

Here is something that neither Secretary Stevens nor I had much to do with. The charge by the Junior Senator from Wisconsin that we've had another year of treason under President Eisenhower, the charge that the CIA is infiltrated and infested with Communists, the charge that the Department of Defense is full of Communists, the charge that the Department of Justice, that the Attorney General of the Department of Justice—there's something phony about him—and the charge that the hydrogen bomb plants and the atomic bomb plants are full of Communists. Well, where do we go from here as the American people? It would appear some of us want to end up in this country with just plain anarchy.

MCCARTHY

Will he, Symington, be willing to go under oath the same as the rest of us are going under oath, the same as I have gone under oath and will go under oath, the same as Republicans have gone under oath, and tell us the truth of what part he had to play with this? If he will merely consent to go on the stand and tell us why and how it happened that, number one, he got the political advisor of the Democrat Party to guide undercover the Republican Secretary of the Army, and, number two, while our friend sanctimonious Stu—

SYMINGTON

Very frankly, I resent that reference to my first name.

MCCARTHY

Advising—

SYMINGTON

You ought to, you ought to go to a psychiatrist, and I want no psychological bribes from you. Nobody in the Senate knows more about how to avoid testifying than the Junior Senator from Wisconsin. And everybody in the United States knows that that fact is true. There've been times when they wanted to put you under oath and you didn't want to go.

MCCARTHY

Mr. Symington has said that no one knows better than the Senator from Wisconsin how to avoid testifying. I have now, at this time, made the offer to go on the stand and let him question me about everything—I don't care how irrelevant it is.

SYMINGTON

"Mr. Chairman. I have decided to testify under oath before this Committee. I believe that I will have performed a public service of overwhelming importance if any action of mine can induce you to answer under oath the allegations formally preferred against you by the Senate Subcommittee, and to which you have heretofore persistently refused to respond except to denounce the Subcommittee. Accordingly, I propose that we agree on the following points: one, you will agree to an investigation by a Committee of the Senate; I will agree to take the stand in the present proceedings and to testify as to the events preceding the institution of these hearings. I trust that you will confirm your agreement with this program. If you are in accord, please sign as indicated below."
Senator, here's the letter and if you will sign it, maybe we can get this matter settled.

McCARTHY

Mr. Chairman—Mr. Symington, I think, and I'm glad we're on television. I think that the millions of people can see how low that a man can sink. I repeat, they can see how low an alleged man can sink. He's been asked here to come before the Committee and give the information which he has in regard to this investigation. He retorts by saying that he wants all of the old smears investigated. Now may I say this, Mr. Chairman. If that is necesary in order to get Symington on the stand, that will be done.

SYMINGTON

All you have to do is sign it.

McCARTHY

Don't pull that phony thing on me.

SYMINGTON

Sign the letter. There it is Senator, it's got my signature on it.

McCARTHY

You have a document with false statements in it. I will not sign and agree that it's true. Don't—you're not fooling anyone, Mr. Symington. You're not fooling anyone. I have offered to go before any committee, do anything you ask, if I can just get you to come down here and take the oath so we can get the answers to some questions. You're, you're not fooling anyone at all.

SYMINGTON

Senator.

McCARTHY

I'm sure of that.

SYMINGTON

Senator, let me tell you something. The American people have had a look at you for six weeks. You're not fooling anyone either.

SYMINGTON

May I ask you to prepare a list for me, Mr. Carr, showing the persons of all categories who have free access to Committee files and the approximate number involved in each category?

CARR

I could do that for you right now, if you want to take the time.

SYMINGTON

All right, fine.

CARR

The Committee members have access to the file, free access to the files. I, as Staff Director, have free access to the files.

SYMINGTON

Who is that? Who is that?

CARR

I do myself, Mr. Cohn does, Mr. Kennedy does, Mr.—the rest of the legal counsel and investigators do, and my secretary or Mr. Cohn's secretary would have access to the files if they went down there for me. The access would be through the file clerk. However, I don't preclude the possibility that if the file clerk wasn't there, they could physically find the file.

SYMINGTON

And it really wouldn't make any difference whether one had top secret and all the rest had secret, or one had secret and all the rest had top secret, if they all had access to the files. Isn't that right?

CARR

Uh, I would, I would say that it wouldn't, uh, make a great deal of difference whether it was secret or top secret, no.

SYMINGTON

It would be unfortunate if we had a subversive on our staff and he hadn't had clearance, and then he examined an agency, and in that agency he got information which made it possible for him to betray the country.

CARR

It would be unfortunate and it would be most unusual. We don't have any subversives on our staff.

SYMINGTON

Well, Klaus Fuchs—was unusual, wasn't he? And so was Mr. May.

CARR

He certainly was.

SYMINGTON

Now, Mr. Carr, under the present rules for access to files of this Committee, if a former Communist who hadn't really reformed, or a subversive, or any security risk on this Committee's staff, that might get on it, decided to betray his country by revealing the contents of a secret FBI document which he had found in these files, based to a possible enemy, it would be a relatively simple matter, would it not, for him to do that, based on the way these files are handled?

MCCARTHY

Mr. Chairman.

SYMINGTON

Would you answer the question and then we're going to go to vote.

MUNDT

Will the witness answer the question.

MCCARTHY

May I ask a personal privilege, Mr. Chairman, to ask one question? I do want to raise that point before we leave this afternoon.

MUNDT

Well, raise it quickly because we're going to have to adjourn for the vote.

MCCARTHY

I will raise it as briefly as I can. May I say that Senator Symington has been here by innuendo trying to smear this staff of young men who have been working to dig out Communists. He's talking about what might happen if there were a subversive on the staff. I would like to ask him now, even though he's not under oath, whether he has any information at all of any kind to justify this attempted smear against these fourteen young men who have done such an excellent job on covering Communists. If he has no information, then he should be honest enough to tell us. If he has information, he should take the stand and take the oath as these young have been taking it. Now may I ask you, Senator, do you have any information to indicate that there is anyone on my staff who is subversive, as you have indicated in your questioning?

MUNDT

Senator Symington, will you answer the question, and then we're going to have recess for the voting.

SYMINGTON

I will answer that question this way, Senator McCarthy. In all the years that I have been in this government, based on the testimony that's been given before this Committee under oath, I think the files of what you call "my staff," "my director," "my chief of staff," have been the sloppiest and most dangerously handled files that I have ever known of since I've been in the government. [*Applause.*]

MUNDT

Recess until 10:00 o'clock.

MCCARTHY

Mr. Chairman. You can run away if you like, Stu, you can run away if you like. You have been here trying to smear the staff of this Committee, the young men who have been working to uncover Communists—you jump up and run away without answering the question. I have asked you a simple question. Do you have, do you have any evidence of any kind to indicate that there's a subversive amongst these young men? If not, if not, you are leaving here this afternoon, leaving a smear upon the name of each and every one of them. You shouldn't do that, Mr. Symington. That's just dishonest. That's, that's the same thing that the Communist Party has been doing—too long.

SYMINGTON

Apparently every time anybody says anything against anybody working for Senator McCarthy, he's smearing them and accusing them of Communism. [*Stands up and prepares to leave committee room.*]

McCARTHY

Just answer the question. Are there any subversives? [*Laughter.*] Mr. Chairman, Mr. Chairman. Even though the Chair—I want to make this record, and Mr. Reporter, will, Mr. Reporter, will you take this down? Mr. Symington and other members of the Democrat Party here, have been intimating that they know of some subversives on this staff investigating Communists. I have asked Mr. Symington point blank to tell us whether he knew of any such subversive. He runs away. He won't answer the question. May I say that that is the most dishonest, the most unfounded smear upon some of the most outstanding young men that I have ever seen work to uncover Communists, and before this is over, the American people will have a better picture of it. I guess we must go and vote now.

Epilogue

Joseph R. McCarthy died May 2, 1957. The three years after the Army-McCarthy Hearings ended were all rather consistently and decisively downhill. He never regained his former menace. And without the menace, the remaining elements of McCarthy and McCarthyism hardly hung together at all.

There has been some excessive delicacy in referring to the circumstance, but the truth of the matter (widely known and appreciated in Washington) is that the man was drinking excessively. Indeed, he died of it—unless one wants to say that he died rather of whatever it was that led him to drink so much. If the latter, then one can say that he died of not being the real *Joe McCarthy any longer (or perhaps having to live too close to the really real one). In any event, he was never the same Joe McCarthy after the Hearings. The camera had done its deadly work too well.*

In a formal way, four reports issued from the Hearings on September 1, 1954—a Republican, a Democratic, and two separate statements by Senators Potter and Dirksen. They were diffuse in effect—and in any event unequal to the task of telling the American people what it had found out for itself via television. Also, before the formal reports were released, Roy Cohn had resigned as chief counsel and Senator Ralph Flanders had introduced in the Senate a resolution of censure against McCarthy. After debate, a Select Committee was authorized to consider the censure motion. The chairman named was the Republican Arthur V. Watkins. The Watkins Committee, as it came to be known, conducted hearings of a much more rigorous nature than those involving the Army. Under the firm direction of his counsel, Edward Bennett Williams, McCarthy was fairly well-behaved before the Watkins Committee—there was not much effort to adapt Senate floor rules to his own purposes, as in the Army Hearings, with frequent points of order. The Select Committee, in a forty thousand-word report, recommended censure and on December 2, 1954, the Senate voted, 67 to 22, to censure its colleague from Wisconsin. The grounds were more limited than those originally proposed, but significant enough for all that. His previous influence in the Senate was at an end.

But he never lost his hard-core followers in the country. At his death, some of them more or less accused the President of his murder. It was that extreme. As the irresistable force it was when the Hearings began in 1954, McCarthyism is dead along with Joe McCarthy. But many of the substantial elements thereof, now strongly reconstituted, are still very much alive today.

In Robert's Rules *of parliamentary procedure, a "point of order" is defined in this way: "One 'makes a point of order' when he objects to a proceeding as being out of order," which it is "when the rules are violated." In a sense, Joe McCarthy's whole life was one loud scream—*"Point of order, Mr. Chairman!" *His eternal followers in their millions, with lives and views of life based on bygone rules which no chairman can any longer observe, are still screaming their objection to the proceedings "as being out of order." For them, they truly are—and will be. History is the "proceedings" and the "rules" are the verities of the past. For a poor humanity engaged in swift history, a point of order is always tragically relevant.*

"Point of order, Mr. Chairman!"

—DAVID T. BAZELON